World of Music

Europe

Patrick Allen

www.heinemann.co.uk/library
Visit our website to find out more information about **Heinemann Library** books.

To order:
 Phone 44 (0)1865 888066
 Send a fax to 44 (0)1865 314091
Visit the Heinemann Bookshop at www.heinemann.co.uk/library to browse our catalogue and order online.

First published in Great Britain by Heinemann Library, Halley Court, Jordan Hill, Oxford OX2 8EJ, part of Harcourt Education. Heinemann is a registered trademark of Harcourt Education Ltd.

© Harcourt Education Ltd 2008

Editorial: Louise Galpine, Harriet Milles, and
        Rachel Howells
Design: Victoria Bevan and Philippa Baile
Illustrations: Jeff Edwards
Picture Research: Hannah Taylor and Fiona Orbell
Production: Julie Carter

Originated by Chroma Graphics (Overseas) Pte Ltd
Printed and bound in China

ISBN 978 0 4311 1776 8
12 11 10 09 08
10 9 8 7 6 5 4 3 2 1

British Library Cataloguing in Publication Data
Allen, Patrick
Europe. – (World of Music)
780.9'4
A full catalogue record for this book is available from the British Library.

Acknowledgements

The publishers would like to thank the following for permission to reproduce photographs: Alamy Images pp. **6** (Terry Harris just greece photo library), **23** (Lebrecht Music & Arts Photo Library), **29** (Tiit Veermae), **33** (Keith Dannemiller), **43** (Pictorial Press Ltd); Bridgeman Art Library pp. **12** (British Library, London, UK), **30–31** (Koninklijk Museum voor Schone Kunsten, Antwerp, Belgium); Corbis pp. **7** (epa/Urs Flueeler), **8** (Geoffrey Clements), **9** (Stapleton Collection), **10–11** (Robbie Jack), **13** (Andy Warhol Foundation), **14** (Bettmann), **17** (Neal Preston), **20** (Free Agents Limited), **21** (Richard Klune), **22** (Brooke Fasani), **25** (epa/ Martial Trezzini), **35** (Robbie Jack), **36** (The Art Archive), **39** (zefa/Hugh Sitton), **40** (Reuters/ Toby Melville), **41** (Reuters/Gleb Garanich); Getty Images pp. **18** (Hulton Archive), **24** (Jim Dyson), **38** (Getty Images/Mario Tama); Lebrecht pp. **5** (Vicky Alhadeff), **16** (David Farrell); Redferns pp. **15** (Erica Echenberg), **19** (David Redfern), **26–27** (Ross Gilmore), **28** (Suzie Gibbons), **32** (Nicky J. Sims), **34** (Phil Dent), **37** (BBC Photo Library); Topfoto/ ArenaPAL/Pete Jones p. **42**

Cover photograph of traditional accordion player, Austria, reproduced with permission of Getty Images/LOOK.

Disclaimer

Contents

Some words will be printed in bold, **like this.** You can find out what they mean by looking in the glossary.

Welcome to European music

The music of Europe is rich and varied. Many Europeans still play and sing the **folk music** of their communities, which has been handed down over thousands of years. Europe is also the home of the **orchestra** and **classical music**, as well as famous **composers** like Mozart. Recently, the continent has produced some of the world's most famous pop musicians, such as the Beatles and the Rolling Stones.

Europe is made up of many nations and the people speak a variety of languages. Switzerland's music and language come from French, German, and Italian traditions. In a similar way, music from the **Celtic** people can be found all down the Atlantic coast in different countries, including Britain, Ireland, France, and Spain.

The music of Europe has not just stayed in Europe. Between the 16th and 20th centuries Europeans explored distant lands and built vast **empires**. European culture and music spread all over the world. Even the United States was built from 13 British **colonies**. Now in the 21st century, people and ideas from the former colonies are having a big influence on the music of Europe.

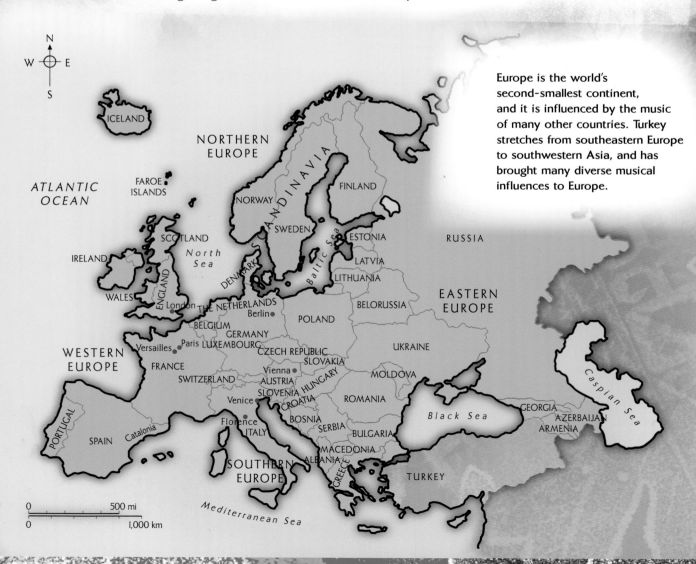

Europe is the world's second-smallest continent, and it is influenced by the music of many other countries. Turkey stretches from southeastern Europe to southwestern Asia, and has brought many diverse musical influences to Europe.

Music has always been part of work, entertainment, and worship. Two thousand years ago Europe was a **pagan** continent where many gods were worshipped. Gradually **Christianity** spread across most regions of Europe. However, some parts of Europe, like Spain, were influenced by the life and music of another religion, **Islam**. Modern instruments like the guitar and the violin are the result of this Islamic influence.

Trade and technology made Europe more wealthy. Great wealth, however, was in the hands of relatively few. These very rich people paid for the first orchestras and composers to entertain their guests, and to show how wealthy they were.

Sharon Corr plays the violin for Irish folk rock band, The Corrs. She is pictured here at Proms in the Park, London, in 2004.

Folk music in Europe

Each group of European people is proud of its ancient folk music traditions. In the warm south of Europe, the folk music can be very passionate and energetic. Some Greek singers and dancers will break plates, even over their heads, to fully express *kefi*, which means joy, passion, pain, and frenzy. On the Greek island of Ikaria there are many outdoor festivals of music and dancing during the summer, celebrating the name days of **saints**.

In the colder north of Europe there has been a long tradition of telling stories through song, to pass the long winter evenings. These "story songs" are called **ballads**. In the Faroe Islands, midway between Iceland, Norway, and Scotland, a tradition of singing, chanting, and dancing to ballads has survived. Some singers can remember up to 350 verses!

These Greek men are performing a dance called *Sirtáki*. *Sirtáki* is danced in a line or circle. The dance begins with slow actions, but gradually gets faster, often including hops and leaps.

These alphorn players from Switzerland are performing a concert on Rigi mountain. The alphorn's mellow sound is produced by vibrations from the players' lips. The sound can carry for very long distances.

In the mountainous Alpine region of central Europe, people sent messages across mountain valleys using rapid voice changes from high to low **pitches**. This developed into a style of singing known as **yodelling**. This style has since travelled all over the world, even into American country music. The huge **alphorn**, now a musical instrument, was also originally used as a way of sending messages. Some measure up to 4 metres (12 feet) in length.

In the west of Europe along the edges of the Atlantic coastline, the Celtic communities share musical traditions. The dances and **bagpipes** of the Irish and Scots are well known around the world. Similar traditions also exist in Brittany (France) and Galicia and Asturias (Spain). These areas were linked by sea trading and travel for thousands of years.

Russian rap

In eastern Europe the largest country is Russia. It may surprise you that Russians have performed a kind of rap music for hundreds of years. In Chastushka music, performers "rap" poetry over a musical backing, often as a kind of competition between performers, just like "hip hop".

Music and religion

Europeans once worshipped many different gods. Scenes of music making and dance during festivals dedicated to gods and goddesses were painted on ancient Greek pots and vases.

From about the 4th century CE (about 1,700 years ago) most of Europe became Christian. Early Christians developed a simple and beautiful style of singing religious words called **plainchant**, which is still performed today. Gradually cathedrals and monasteries formed choirs to sing more complicated pieces.

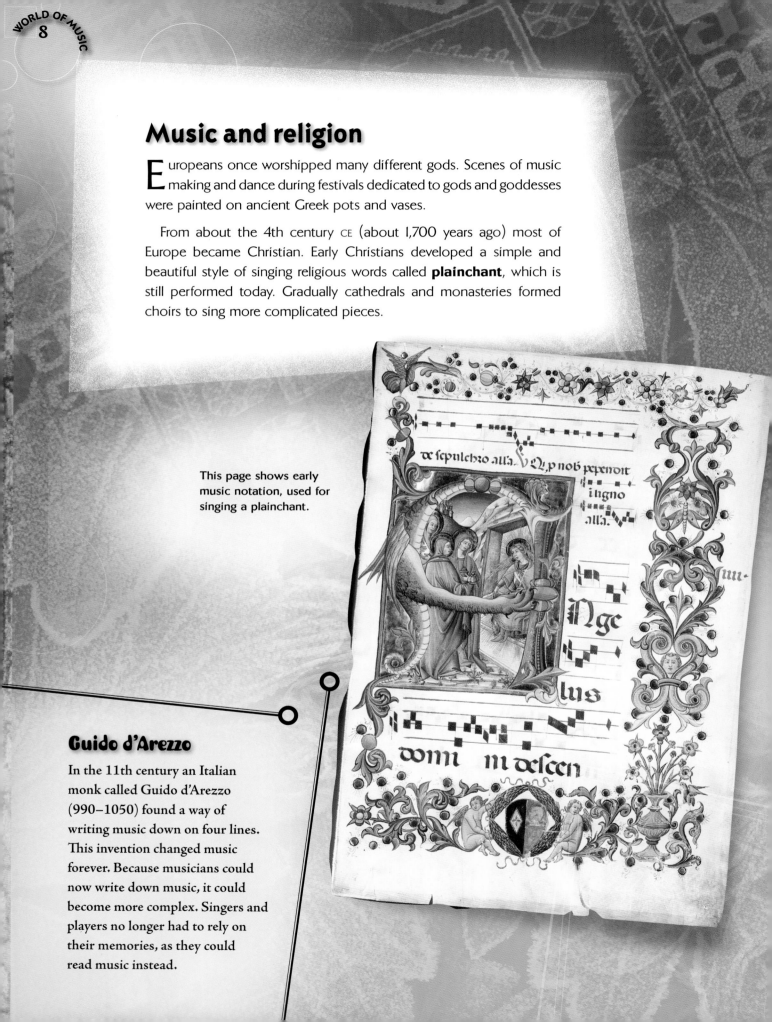

This page shows early music notation, used for singing a plainchant.

Guido d'Arezzo

In the 11th century an Italian monk called Guido d'Arezzo (990–1050) found a way of writing music down on four lines. This invention changed music forever. Because musicians could now write down music, it could become more complex. Singers and players no longer had to rely on their memories, as they could read music instead.

As the Church became richer it employed the best musicians to write complicated pieces, but the music became too difficult for ordinary people to sing. The **Protestant** Christians of northern Europe encouraged composers to write simple "hymns" for the people to sing. These hymns are still sung all over the world.

Some larger churches remained very wealthy and paid for the best composers to write music, and for the most skilled musicians to play it. Many great composers including Bach, Mozart, and Beethoven have written music for the Church, which is still performed today.

Banned bands

In 18th-century England, churches had bands and choirs of local people to lead the music. The bands were sometimes noisy and difficult for church leaders to control. After an argument the bands would sometimes refuse to play! This encouraged churches to replace the bands with organs in the 19th century, which needed just one player.

This painting, by Thomas Weber, shows an English village choir and band. It is called *The Village Choir*, and was painted in 1847.

Hildegard of Bingen

Hildegard of Bingen (1098–1179) was a German nun, and one of the earliest women composers. She wrote beautiful plainchant which is still sung and recorded today. She lived in a **convent** for 70 years. She was known as a wise woman, and was visited in her cell by kings and princes.

European classical music

Classical music has usually been composed, written down, and performed by professional musicians. Professional musicians are often trained and are paid to perform and compose music. For hundreds of years musicians would entertain the guests of the wealthy and provide music for singing and dancing.

During the 16th century music became more complicated, and players and singers more skilled. In Italy, wealthy families like the Medicis of Florence paid **composers** to produce startling new pieces that would impress their guests. These pieces became part of amazing stage shows that could sometimes last over two days!

This opera singer is performing the part of the Queen of the Night from Mozart's opera *The Magic Flute*.

The orchestra

During the 17th century the rich began to pay for **orchestras** to entertain them. An orchestra is a large team of instrumental players. Most of the instruments in an orchestra are string instruments, such as violins. They are joined by **woodwind** instruments, such as the flute, and **brass** instruments, such as the trumpet. This is an expensive way of making music, since each orchestra requires a large team of skilled musicians.

The German-born composer Johann Sebastian Bach was given a job as a *kapellmeister* or court musician. This role involved writing, rehearsing, and performing an enormous amount of music both for the rich family that employed him, and the local church. As well as composing thousands of long pieces of music Bach also had 20 children!

Oldest operas

Opera tells a story entirely in song. The first opera, performed in 1597, was *Dafne* by a composer called Peri. Unfortunately most of *Dafne* has been lost, so the oldest complete, surviving opera that is still performed is *Orfeo* by Monteverdi. *Orfeo* was first performed in 1607. In the 17th century opera began to move out of private homes and into public theatres. The audiences could be very noisy and would use the occasion for meeting their friends, often shouting and eating during the performance!

Antonio Vivaldi

A famous composer from the period known as the Baroque (1610–1750) was the Italian Antonio Vivaldi (1678–1741). His famous piece *The Four Seasons* describes each season in vivid music. The piece has been widely used in the media and even in video games.

From Mozart to Stockhausen

During the 18th century, the orchestra grew in size, and included new instruments like the **clarinet**. The most famous composers of the period were the Austrians named Franz Haydn and Wolfgang Amadeus Mozart.

This picture shows Mozart at a young age. Mozart is playing the piano, while his father plays the violin and his sister sings.

Wolfgang Amadeus Mozart

Wolfgang Amadeus Mozart (1756–1791) was a child prodigy. Before the age of seven he had toured Europe, performing to kings, queens, and princes and composed many pieces for piano, violin, and organ. He had an amazing musical memory. As a child he wrote down a 5-minute long piece of music after hearing it only once. Despite only living to the age of 35 he composed over 50 symphonies, about 50 concertos, and 24 operas. His music, such as *Eine Kleine Nachtmusik* and the *Requiem*, is some of the most famous in the world.

Dark beginnings

We are used to the **auditorium** being darkened in theatres. It first happened in 1876 in the opera house in Bayreuth, Germany, which was built to perform the operas of Wagner. This helped the audience to concentrate on the music.

This portrait of Beethoven was painted by Andy Warhol, an American artist who became famous for his unusual art in the 1960s.

During the 19th century composers began to write to express their own feelings rather than simply entertain the guests of the wealthy. The growing number of concert halls meant that the general public could support musicians by paying to go to their concerts. The music of this time is far more dramatic and emotional than before. Composers like the Polish pianist Chopin and the Russian composer Tchaikovsky were important composers of this period.

Ludwig van Beethoven

The German musician Ludwig van Beethoven (1770–1827) was a brilliant pianist and probably the most famous composer of all time. He is best known for his piano music and symphonies. He began to go deaf at the age of 28. By the time he wrote the majestic *Ninth Symphony* he was completely deaf.

Entertainment and popular music

Until the 19th century, most Europeans lived in the countryside. Their music was often centred around farming and the land.

The **Industrial Revolution** began in Britain and soon spread to the whole of Europe. It meant that many people moved from the countryside into the expanding towns for work. Sometimes people adapted a country tradition for the town. In Paris, France, a style of **accordion** music called *Bal Musette* developed as country people brought their dance music to the city.

The **mass production** of musical instruments in the 19th century meant that ordinary people could buy them. Coal-miners and factory workers in Britain even formed **brass** bands, consisting mainly of brass instruments, such as trumpets and trombones. These bands still exist today, and perform to a very high standard. Lively pub entertainment developed into a musical variety show known as Music Hall. The audiences were loud, shouting at the stage and singing along to songs like *Daisy Bell* and *My Old Man*. Music Hall singer Marie Lloyd sang the "pop" hits of her day.

This picture shows the French singer Edith Piaf in 1955. She was very small in size, but had a powerful singing voice.

Edith Piaf

In Paris, Berlin, and other large cities, nightclubs began to open in the early 20th century. Edith Piaf (1915–1963) was the most famous French nightclub singer of this time. She had a powerful voice, despite being tiny. She was only 1.4 metres (4 feet 8 inches) tall and known as the "Little Sparrow". She began her career singing for pennies on street corners and ended it as the most famous woman in France.

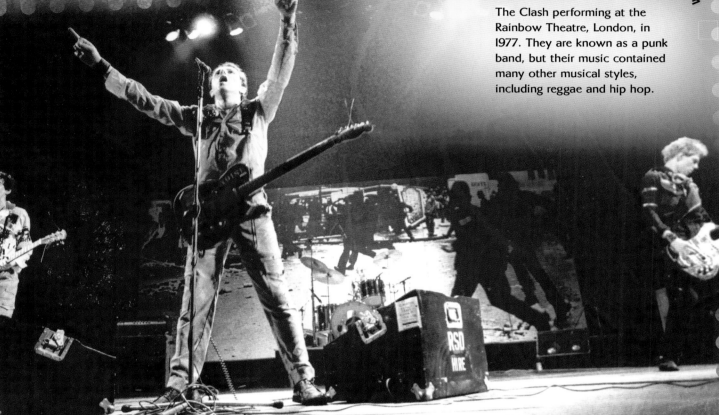

The Clash performing at the Rainbow Theatre, London, in 1977. They are known as a punk band, but their music contained many other musical styles, including reggae and hip hop.

In the 1970s the young people of European cities, especially in Britain, started making aggressive home-made rock music and dressing in shocking clothes. This punk music was based on an American style, but soon became something new. The Clash were one of the most famous punk bands. In 1976 the band started performing their style of raw, politically-charged rock in London clubs and pubs with audiences "pogoing" (jumping up and down) to their songs. Their music contains many influences, including **reggae**, a style of music from Jamaica. This music had come to London in the 1950s with Jamaicans who came to live in British cities.

Popular music – bands

In the mid 20th century, Europeans could hear music from distant places through recordings and radio. Britain has a shared history and culture with the United States going back more than 400 years. European countries welcomed American popular music styles like "rock 'n' roll" and "the blues" and began to produce their own bands and new styles of pop music.

The Rolling Stones, Led Zeppelin, Queen, and The Who are a few of the world famous bands who came out of Britain in the 1960s and 1970s. Bands like the Beatles and the Kinks developed a very "English" sound. These bands were so successful that they had a big influence on American music. This exchange of ideas continues to this day.

The Beatles

The Beatles (pictured left to right: Paul McCartney, George Harrison, Ringo Starr, and John Lennon) were four ordinary boys from Liverpool, England. They began playing in a Liverpool club called The Cavern in the early 1960s. The Beatles became the best-selling recording artists of the 20th century, composing some of the biggest hits of all time such as *Let It Be* and *She Loves You*. The group broke up in 1970.

Styles such as heavy metal and glam rock also originated in Britain. Heavy metal music is a powerful and dramatic style of rock. Bands like Black Sabbath and Deep Purple are typical heavy metal bands.

Glam rock was a lively style of rock music from the early 1970s, which also involved the wearing of glittery costumes! David Bowie, Elton John, and the Sweet began as chart-topping glam rock performers. Glam rock bands like Roxy Music experimented with new musical styles.

The heavy metal band Deep Purple are shown here, performing in 1973. The Guinness Book of World Records once had them listed as the world's loudest band! Deep Purple are still together today.

Popular music in other European countries was often influenced by local **folk music**. In northern Europe a light pop style called *schlager* (German for "hits"), based on folk music, remains very popular. The Swedish band Abba began writing and performing in this style. They mixed the catchy tunes and harmonies of the *schlager* style with disco beats. This combination took them to worldwide fame in the 1970s and 1980s.

Pop stars

French-speaking European countries, such as France, Belgium, and Switzerland, developed a unique style of pop singing called *chanson* (French for "song"). In these songs the words, the emotions, and the personal stories are more important than the melody. The Belgian singer-songwriter Jacques Brel was a master of this style. He was very popular in the 1960s and 1970s and his songs have been translated into fifteen languages.

Belgian singer and composer Jacques Brel performing for French television. Brel also made a career of acting and directing films.

Julio Iglesias is the best-selling Spanish singing star of all time, having sold 250 million records worldwide. He was a professional footballer, but after an injury in a car accident, decided to try singing. His music combines Spanish styles with "Latino" **rhythms** from the Americas.

Björk is a singer from Iceland in the far north of Europe. Iceland is a small country with only 300,000 people. Björk (which means "Birch tree" in Icelandic) has become famous around the world since her first solo recording in 1993. Her music is original and sometimes unusual. She began as a punk singer but then developed her own style of song-writing and performing.

English singer-songwriters like David Bowie, Sting, and Elton John are also world famous. Elton John (real name Reginald Kenneth Dwight) composes and performs from the piano. He has produced international hits like *Rocket Man* as well as songs for Disney's *The Lion King* including *Can You Feel the Love Tonight?* He originally wrote *Candle in the Wind* in 1973, as a **tribute** to Marilyn Monroe. Elton rewrote the song to perform at the funeral of Diana, Princess of Wales in 1997.

This picture shows Nana Mouskouri in concert. She spoke many different languages, which allowed her to reach audiences all over Europe, the United States, and Asia.

Nana Mouskouri

Greek singer Nana Mouskouri, who was born in 1934, has a bright and clear singing voice. She became a worldwide celebrity in the late 20th century and helped make Greek music known around the world. She was also famous for making the wearing of glasses glamorous! She was elected to the European Parliament in 1994. This assembly represents the views of people from all over Europe.

Musical instruments

The **folk music** of Europe is played using instruments that became available to musicians in their communities long ago. European musicians have always been open to new ideas and have often borrowed musical ideas and instruments from other cultures. Some folk instruments are associated with particular places, but actually have their origins elsewhere.

Are bagpipes Scottish?

Bagpipes use a bag to store air (so there is a constant supply of air) and a stick with holes called a "chanter" to play the melody. They also have a drone (a constant note that plays underneath the tune). The bagpiper wearing a kilt is a popular image of Scotland. However, bagpipes can be found all over the world and were first written about in Egypt in 100 BCE. In Bulgaria they are so popular that it is said "a wedding without bagpipes is like a funeral". They have also remained popular in the **Celtic** regions of Europe, especially Asturias in Spain where the pipes (or *gaita*) are almost identical to the Scottish pipes.

This picture shows how traditional Scottish bagpipers dress. Bagpipes are not only played in Scotland - they can be found all over the world.

Are accordions French?

The sound of an **accordion** is made with air from hand-held **bellows**. The air plays reeds which vibrate and make musical notes. The player pushes buttons and piano-style keys. The familiar sound of an accordion playing in a Paris café might make us believe it is a French instrument. However, it was first invented in 1829 in Vienna, Austria and has since been used in folk music all over Europe.

Violins and fiddles

The "fiddle" is a violin played as a folk instrument. It is very popular in the folk dance music of Scandinavia, Ireland, and eastern Europe. The violin has four strings and is played with a bow or plucked. The modern violin was developed in Italy in the 16th century but can trace its origins to the 10th century *rebab*, an Arabic instrument.

Travelling guitars

The modern six-string guitar was developed in Seville, in Spain, in the 19th century by Antonio Torres Jurado. However, the guitar can trace its ancestry in Spain back to the **Moors** who brought a similar instrument from North Africa to Spain, and the Romans who brought a similar Greek instrument to the rest of Europe in the 1st century CE.

These fiddle players from Mora, Sweden, are performing in a midsummer festival.

Orchestral and keyboard instruments

Most modern **orchestral** instruments were developed in Europe. These instruments have been improved over the centuries by craftspeople.

The trumpet

The trumpet started life thousands of years ago when people discovered that the sound of lips vibrating into an animal horn could be very impressive. This big sound was useful for royal occasions and battles. By 1400 BCE the instruments were made of metal, and in around 1440 CE the metal tubes became curved. The earliest trumpets of this type have been found in Germany. Valves were added to trumpets in England and Austria in the early 19th century and this helped players to reach a wider range of notes more easily.

The piano

The piano (or pianoforte) was invented in Italy in the early 18th century by Bartolomeo Cristofori. The piano was a **revolutionary** instrument. It was capable of playing soft (*piano*) and loud (*forte*) sounds. When a key is pressed on the piano a hammer strikes the strings and is then released. This was an improvement on the earlier harpsichord where a mechanism plucked the strings. The piano helped performers to be more expressive in their performances because they could play both loud and soft sounds.

The piano was invented in Europe, but is now played all over the world. This boy is playing his piano in Cape Town, South Africa.

From belt to orchestra

Timpani or kettle drums are large drums capable of making deep and loud sounds. Originally called nakers, they began life in Turkish and Arabic military ceremonies, strapped to the belt of the player who was sometimes on horseback. They were first used in the orchestra in the 17th century.

The saxophone

The saxophone was invented in France around 1840 by Adolphe Sax. The sound is created in the same way as a clarinet. The player blows into a mouthpiece and a single reed vibrates. As it is made of **brass** and is generally larger than the clarinet, the sound is considerably louder. Sax wanted to create a **woodwind** instrument with the power of a brass instrument, suitable for outdoor playing in bands. Its quality of sound has made it popular in jazz and other modern music.

This is John Coltrane, a celebrated American saxophonist. He is performing here at Comblais La Tour, France, in 1963.

Electronic instruments

The earliest successful electronic instrument was the theremin, invented by Russian Leon Theremin around 1920. It is probably the only instrument that is played without being touched. The player moves his hand around two antennae. The electronic sound slides up and down with the movement of the hands. French composer Messiaen, and the Russian composer Stravinsky wrote music for it, but its most famous use is in the Beach Boys' pop hit *Good Vibrations* from 1966.

One of the early music **synthesizers** was developed by the Russian Ivor Darreg between 1937 and 1957. The tape recorder was invented in Germany during World War II. Composers like the German Karl-heinz Stockhausen and Frenchman Pierre Boulez experimented with tape editing and synthesizers to produce electronic music. It was called *Musique Concrète* (concrete music!) because it was music made from "real" sounds, such as humans and the natural world, rather than from musical instruments.

Computers and synthesizers were used in popular music in the 1970s and 1980s. Rock bands, such as the English band Pink Floyd, experimented with electronic music in the 1960s, but the pioneers of "total" electronic music were German band Kraftwerk (*Kraftwerk* is the German word for power station). Their classic album *Autobahn* (1974) introduced the world to electronic beats and catchy synthesizer backings.

This theremin player is performing at a concert in London. The theremin produces a unique sound, which has been used in films to create a spooky atmosphere.

In the 1980s computers were used to control synthesizers. British "synthpop" bands like the Human League and the Eurythmics built on Kraftwerk's style to produce worldwide electronic hits. They changed the way pop music was made by completely replacing "real" instruments with electronic ones.

German band Kraftwerk performing in Switzerland in 2005. They invented much of what we now know as modern electronic music.

Jean Michel Jarre

French performer and composer Jean Michel Jarre (born 1948) has produced electronic hits on a grander scale, beginning with his famous *Oxygène* albums from the late 1970s. Jarre creates a warm sound and grand effects, and his music is some of the most popular electronic music ever written. His stage shows were equally magnificent, using banks of lights and lasers in grand locations, such as Tiananmen Square in China and in Houston, Texas, where he performed to a worldwide television audience of 1.5 million.

The Voice

Professional singers and songwriters have made a living with their voices for thousands of years.

In Medieval Europe (400–1400 CE), minstrels were professional singer-songwriters who wrote **ballads** and love songs to be sung in the homes of the wealthy. Some minstrels were permanent employees, but most travelled between clients, and would perform on their travels to raise extra money. Sometimes the minstrel would be part of a team of musicians in a wealthy house.

In Britain, ballads were sung in pubs and homes by ordinary people and professionals. After the invention of the printing press in the 15th century, a huge trade in printed ballads began in England. Songwriters would compose ballads about current events, politics, murders, and mysteries, which would then go on sale to the general public. Known as "broadside ballads" they were a fun way of spreading news.

Opera superstars

Amongst the wealthy people of 18th-century Europe it was opera singers who were the superstars of their day. Counts, kings, and princes would spend small fortunes to hear these singers. For example, the famous opera singer Farinelli was paid to stay for 10 years in Spain to help cure King Philip of depression. Queen Christina of Sweden stopped a war between Sweden and Poland just so she could hear the singer Ferri perform.

This is the world's most famous *fado* star, Mariza. Mariza was born in Mozambique, Africa, but grew up in Portugal, where *fado* music developed. This performance took place in Glasgow, Scotland, in 2004.

In the 19th century, many people learned to sing and play the piano, and short songs were written for performance in people's homes. The Austrian composer Franz Schubert managed to set 600 poems to music, even though he died at the early age of 31.

In Portugal, a style of professional singing developed from the lives and music of the poor. *Fado* (which means "fate") is a style of passionate singing with links to Arabic and Brazilian music. The music is sung freely and to the accompaniment of a guitar. *Fado* remains very popular to this day and can be heard in cafés and bars as well as concert halls in Portugal.

Singing together

All over Europe people from choral societies sing music composed for choirs. Choral music has been composed in Europe for 500 years. One of the most popular choral pieces is the *Messiah* by Handel, which contains the famous *Hallelujah!* chorus.

Handel was a German musician, working in England, but the first performance of the *Messiah* was in Ireland in 1742. The audience always stand for the *Hallelujah!* chorus in Handel's *Messiah*. This is because King George II of England is said to have been so moved that he rose to his feet when he first heard it. The *Messiah* is still performed all over Europe.

This picture shows the women's choir, *le Mystere des Voix Bulgares*, in concert in London. They have made the Bulgarian folk song famous throughout Europe, the United States, and Asia.

Other parts of Europe have community singing traditions, where complicated music is handed down by ear and not on paper. The musicians learn the pieces by listening and copying. One such tradition is in Georgia in eastern Europe. Here the men meet to sing complicated and powerful songs in harmony. This means they all sing different notes, but they sound good together. Some are love songs and some are "table" or toast songs which accompany drinking. The sound is loud and suitable for outdoors. Some songs are even sung on horseback.

In Bulgaria, it is the women who sing together. The women also sing in harmony and with a strong piercing tone. Some Bulgarian women's choirs are world famous, particularly a choir called *le Mystere des Voix Bulgares*, who have a number of best-selling albums. The American singer Linda Ronstadt described the music of the choir as the "most wonderful music I have ever heard".

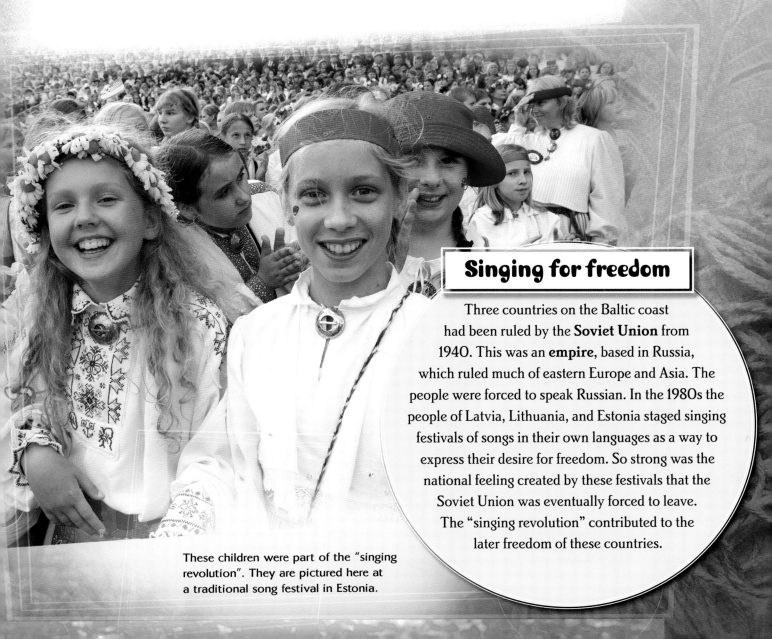

Singing for freedom

Three countries on the Baltic coast had been ruled by the **Soviet Union** from 1940. This was an **empire**, based in Russia, which ruled much of eastern Europe and Asia. The people were forced to speak Russian. In the 1980s the people of Latvia, Lithuania, and Estonia staged singing festivals of songs in their own languages as a way to express their desire for freedom. So strong was the national feeling created by these festivals that the Soviet Union was eventually forced to leave. The "singing revolution" contributed to the later freedom of these countries.

These children were part of the "singing revolution". They are pictured here at a traditional song festival in Estonia.

The language of European music

A **scale** (or "mode") is a sequence of notes, which gives music its character. The world has a huge variety of scales, many of which can sound odd.

European scales of seven different notes (for example CDEFGAB) were established in ancient Greece and are the foundation of most European and western music. By choosing a different starting note the music is given a different feeling. The keyboard, which is used on organs, pianos, **accordions**, and **synthesizers**, clearly shows all the notes and scales available. It was invented in Europe in the 15th century.

The two most widely used scales, the major and the minor scales, were developed in 17th-century Europe. The major key tends to sound cheerful. For example, the U.S national anthem is in a major key. Music in a minor key tends to sound sad. The spiritual *Joshua Fought the Battle of Jericho* is in a minor key.

This 15th-century painting shows angels performing on trumpets, an organ, harp, and violin.

Johann Pachelbel

In the 17th century the German composer Johann Pachelbel (1653–1706) wrote a piece of music called the *Canon in D*. It uses a sequence of eight chords that have been used or adapted in many pop songs. Artists such as Green Day, Coolio, the Beatles, and the Backstreet Boys have used this sequence.

In the 17th century European musicians developed two musical ideas that are still used all over the world:

◎ Keys – the idea that music has a main or key note to which the piece of music must regularly return.

◎ Chord sequences – every pop song is made from a sequence of chords. A chord is a group of notes (usually three) that sound good together when played at the same time. The idea of using a sequence of chords to compose music was developed in Europe in the 17th century. Incredibly, chord sequences established at that time are still in use today.

Rocking rhythms: Let the people dance

The **rhythms** of European music have always inspired people to dance.

In Ireland the ceilidh is an occasion when musicians play energetic dance music such as **jigs** and **reels** for community dancing. Lively Irish "step" dancing and its music have become world-famous through the *Riverdance* films, shows, and recordings. The top half of the body is held still while the legs move quickly. The Chieftains (shown below) are playing the flute, bodhran (Irish drum), guitar, and fiddle. This is a typical Irish dance band.

In the 16th century, European composers wrote dances and arranged them for bands to play for royal celebrations. The *pavane*, a slow and stately dance, allowed the guests to greet each other formally. It was followed by the lively *galliard*, where more physical contact was necessary. Partners held each other as they danced, and occasionally the men lifted the women off the floor.

Austria is famous as the home of the waltz and the polka. The waltz began as a folk dance where the beats are grouped in threes. It became the height of fashion in Vienna in the late 18th and 19th centuries.

The waltz was a very fast dance, running at 150 beats per minute. The couples needed to hold each other tight, since the dance consisted entirely of "turns". Composers such as Johann Strauss composed many waltzes, the most famous of which is *The Blue Danube Waltz*.

The Chieftains are a band who have brought traditional Irish music to the attention of the world. In this picture they are performing at Hyde Park, London, in 2000.

The Macarena is a dance, as well as a song. It started in Spain, but it soon travelled the globe. These people are performing the dance in Mexico.

In modern Europe most towns have clubs where young people meet to dance to electronically produced dance music. Clubs are particularly popular in southern Spain where many northern Europeans go for vacations. Dance crazes develop, which are then spread all over Europe. In the 1990s Spanish duo Los Del Rio had a worldwide hit with their dance hit *Macarena*. The song used a fusion of Spanish and Latin American rhythms.

Rocking rhythms: Dance in performance

During the 16th century the cities of Italy, such as Florence and Venice, were becoming very wealthy. The wealthiest people staged spectacular shows for their guests. Dancing by trained dancers, and music to accompany it, became an important part of these spectacles. The style became known as **ballet**.

In 17th-century France, King Louis XIV ("The Sun King") was the richest and most powerful king in the world and was able to spend vast sums of money as he wished. As well as building palaces like Versailles, near Paris, he could spend a fortune on his passion – ballet. He set up training schools for dancers and musicians. As he was a dancer himself, he would often appear on the stage at his court entertainments.

Ballet has since become a major performance art form in Europe and the music composed for it has become famous in its own right. The music written by the Russian composer Tchaikovsky is particularly loved. His *Nutcracker Suite* composed from 1891–1892 is a Christmas favourite, and was used by Walt Disney in his animation *Fantasia*. Another Tchaikovsky ballet **score**, *Swan Lake*, is still very popular.

This is a production of *Swan Lake*. The ballet was first performed in 1877, but it continues to be popular with modern audiences.

Beautiful ballet?

The ballet music written by Igor Stravinsky for the *Rite of Spring* between 1911 and 1913 was quite different. Instead of beautiful melodies it is full of clashing chords and violent rhythms. At its first performance in Paris rioting and fighting broke out in the audience. The music and dancing were so new that people were shocked.

These *Stomp* cast members are shown performing in London in 1998. Before *Stomp* became a successful stage show it was performed on the streets of Brighton, England.

In the 20th century, music theatre presentations, often featuring dance, became popular. Traditional musical shows like *Les Miserables* by Frenchmen Claude-Michel Schönberg and Alain Boublil have had worldwide success, as have more offbeat shows like the British show *Stomp*.

In *Stomp*, the highly skilled cast use items of junk and waste metal to create complicated rhythms and dance routines, as well as tell a story. After opening in London in 1991, the show is still touring the world.

National and international Europe

Europe is made up of many countries. In the early 20th century smaller countries felt they were under threat from larger countries like Russia and Germany. Both the large and small countries used **folk music** to express the identity of their nation.

In Hungary, the **composer** and pianist Béla Bartók wanted to capture the folk music of the countryside before it disappeared. It was exciting music with irregular **rhythms**, high energy, and unusual harmonies. Whilst recording it, he decided to compose music using ideas from Hungarian traditional music. Bartók was then able to compose music in a Hungarian style. This trend was followed all over Europe. For example, in Spain the composer Granados gave his piano pieces the character of Spanish dances.

Here is Béla Bartók, recording a female singer in Transylvania. Transylvania was part of Hungary, but since 1920 it has been part of Romania.

The Pogues performing on the TV show Top of the Pops in 1988. Although the band played traditional Irish instruments, they were also influenced by English punk bands such as The Clash.

Eastern folk

Croatia, in eastern Europe, is one of five countries that used to form a larger country called Yugoslavia. Croatian folk pop has given the young people an opportunity to express their national identity in music. The music has a strong eastern flavour, being heavily influenced by Turkish and Greek music.

Some European countries have become part of larger countries. Catalonia, which was once an independent nation, is now governed by Spain. In the last 50 years there has been a huge revival in Catalan music and language. A community circle dance called the *Sardana*, accompanied by a local band of musicians playing traditional music, has been revived in most towns and villages. The Catalans also have community processions where people dress as *gigantes* (giants) and are accompanied by traditional marching bands.

Since the 1950s there has been a revival of interest in folk music all over Europe. In the late 1960s the English band Fairport Convention made rock arrangements of English folk songs and dances and found their album *Liege and Lief* to be a best-seller. By using folk tunes they hoped to make rock music more "English". This electric folk style spread throughout Europe. In the 1980s and 1990s The Pogues combined an outrageous punk stage act with traditional Irish instruments such as the tin whistle and mandolin. This style of Irish rock has also been popular in the United States.

International influences

Europe's music has long been influenced by cultures beyond its borders. The **Moors** (from North Africa) occupied much of Spain from the 8th to the 15th centuries. They brought with them musical instruments and styles of singing that remain in Spanish music to this day.

In this photo a Jewish *Klezmer* band is preparing to perform in an Eastern European synagogue (Jewish place of worship).

Jewish communities have moved around Europe (often under force) for more than 2,000 years. From around the 15th century a style of lively music for social occasions, such as weddings and celebrations, which we now call *Klezmer*, developed in European Jewish communities. *Klezmer* music is very passionate, and the lead instrument, usually a clarinet or violin, often imitates the voice laughing or weeping. The style we hear today mainly comes from Jews in eastern Europe and Russia.

The **nomadic** Roma people (sometimes known as gypsies) have moved across Europe for more than 1,000 years. Roma music is widespread in eastern Europe. Roma influence (as well as Jewish and Islamic) is also very strong in flamenco, a powerful style of singing, dancing, and guitar playing from southern Spain. The music is full of life and energy. The brightly dressed dancers twist and turn to the sound of guitars, clapping, and **castanets**. The music is lively but sad, as it comes from people who were poor and rejected by some Spaniards.

European countries built up several **empires** between the 16th and 20th centuries. Settlers from the former **colonies** came to live in France, Britain, Spain, and Portugal, bringing music from the Caribbean, Africa, the United States, and from India to Europe. "Crossover" styles have developed. French singer Faudel mixed North African and French music, and in Britain *Bhangra* music, which uses drumming styles from the Punjab region of India, is very popular today.

This picture shows a Spanish Flamenco dancer and guitarist. Spanish gypsies often say that flamenco is "in the blood", meaning they are naturally skilled at performing the music.

Europe today

Many ancient festivals survive in modern Europe. In Seville, Spain, dramatic hooded figures march slowly down a main street to the pulsating beat of a drum band. They carry giant brass crosses, and a boy waves **incense**. In this Christian celebration, a group carry a gigantic statue of Mary, mother of Jesus, surrounded by burning candles. In the distance a brass band plays a slow and solemn tune. These are the Seville "fraternities" or "marching societies" during Holy Week (Easter). The music is slow and sad to represent a funeral procession for Jesus.

The Notting Hill festival is Europe's largest street festival. It takes place in London to celebrate the culture of the Caribbean community. The carnival was first established in the 1960s and has now become one of England's traditions. At the festival, a **steel band** with brightly dressed players is followed by women dancing in gigantic colourful costumes. A **reggae** band with a booming bass line passes on a lorry, while a gospel choir approach in the distance. People of many races mingle and dance to the beat.

A band of drummers plays at the Notting Hill carnival in 2005. Up to one million people attend this event each year.

This was Norway's entry for the Eurovision Song Contest in 2005. The band are called Wig Wam, and they finished ninth out of 24 competitors.

Up to 500 million people each year watch the Eurovision Song Contest, a television competition of popular song. Many European nations compete, as well as nations outside Europe. Each country votes for their favourite songs, which must be specially composed and performed live for the event. Famous winners include Cliff Richard and Abba, but the most striking were the winners from Finland in 2006 – the heavy metal band Lordi.

Some of Europe's largest rock music festivals take place in Germany. *Rock am Ring* is staged at the Nürburgring race track. As well as British bands like the Prodigy, heavy metal band Iron Maiden, and "indie" rock band Radiohead, particular favourites are the German rock band Rammstein. Their hard rock songs, sung entirely in German, have sold 10 million recordings worldwide. The pounding beats of Rammstein's songs are reflected in their name, which means "ramming stone".

Into the future

Between 1914 and 1945 Europe was the centre of two world wars. The effects are still felt today. The wars divided European nations from each other. Between 1945 and 1991 much of eastern Europe (including Poland and East Germany) was cut off from western Europe as it was ruled by the **Soviet Union**, where people had few personal freedoms.

Since World War II most European nations have become part of the European Union (EU). For the first time in many generations Europeans can live and work freely in different countries within the Union. Europe is uniting and leaving behind its divided past. Europe even has its own national anthem called *Ode To Joy*, written by Ludwig van Beethoven. It comes from his Ninth **Symphony**.

This is the European Union Youth Orchestra, one of the world's most famous orchestras. It is special because it has members from all of the European Union countries.

Even though many languages are spoken in Europe, musical ideas have often travelled quickly around the continent. For example, the violin and the piano were used all over Europe very soon after their invention in Italy. The music of Mozart and Beethoven immediately influenced how composers wrote all over Europe. Kraftwerk helped to develop synthpop in Germany, before it moved into Britain and from there across the world.

Some pop artists too have become "European". French singer Sacha Distel, Spanish singer Julio Iglesias, and Greek **synthesizer** composer Vangelis are popular across the continent. From Iceland to Italy and from Sweden to Spain, Europeans are finding strength, unity, and pride in their important contribution to the world of music.

In this picture Petula Clark is performing her hit single *Downtown* on Top of the Pops in 1964.

Petula Clark

English singer Petula Clark (born 1932) has had the longest lasting chart success of any artist in the world – more than 50 years. She is also a true European, recording in French, German, and Italian. Her career began as a child in the 1940s, when she was popular in both Britain and the United States. Moving to France in the 1950s she became a star in France and Belgium. Her huge hit *Downtown* (1964) was released in three languages. The English version made her popular all over the world. She has continued to release chart topping music in Europe, Australia, and the United States well into the 21st century.

A world of music

	String Instruments	Brass Instruments	Wind Instruments
Africa	*oud* (lute), *rebec* (fiddle), *kora* (harp-lute), *ngoni* (harp), musical bow, one-string fiddle	*kakaki* or *wazi* (metal trumpets), horns made from animal horns	*naga*, *nay sodina* (flutes), *arghul*, *gaita* (single-reed instruments), *mizmar* (double-reed instrument)
Australia, Hawaii, and the Pacific	*ukulele* (modern), guitar (modern)		flutes, nose flutes, didgeridoo, conch shell horns
Eastern Asia	*erhu* (fiddle), *dan tranh*, *qin*, *koto*, *gayageum* (derived from *zithers*)	gongs, metallophones, xylophones	*shakuhachi* (flute), *khaen* (mouth organ), *sralai* (reed instrument)
Europe	violin, viola, cello, double bass, mandolin, guitar, lute *zither*, hurdy gurdy (folk instruments)	trumpet, French horn, trombone, tuba	flute, recorder, oboe, clarinet, bassoon, bass **clarinet**, saxophone, **accordion**, **bagpipes**
Latin America and the Caribbean	*berimbau* (musical bow), *guitarrón* (bass guitar), *charango* (mandolin), *vilhuela* (high-**pitched** guitar)	trumpet, saxophone, trombone (salsa instruments)	*bandoneon* (button accordion)
Western Asia	*sitar*, *veena*, *oud*, *dombra*, *doutar*, *tar* (lutes), *rebab*, *kobyz* (fiddles), *sarod*, *santoor*, *sarangi*	trumpets	*bansuri*, *ney* (flutes), *pungi/been* (clarinets), *shehnai*, *sorna* (oboes)

Percussion Instruments	Vocal Styles	Dance Styles
balafon (wooden xylophone), *mbira* (thumb piano), bells, slit drums, friction drums, hourglass drums, conventional drums	open throat singing, Arabic style singing: this is more nasal (in the nose) and includes many trills and ornaments	spiritual dancing, mass dances, team/formation dances, small group and solo dances, modern social dances
drums, slit drums, rattles, clapsticks, gourds, rolled mats	*oli* (sung by one person), *mele* (poetry), hula, *himene* (choral music), Dreaming songs	hula, seated dances, *fa'ataupati* (clapping and singing), haka
taiko (drums)	*p'ansori* (single singer), *chooimsae* (verbal encouragement), folk songs	Peking/Beijing Opera, Korean folk dance
side drum, snare drum, tambourine, *timpani* (kettle drums), cymbals, **castanets**, bodhran, piano	solo **ballad**, work song, hymn, **plainchant**, opera, Music Hall, cabaret, choral, homophony (harmony, parts moving together), polyphony (independent vocals together)	**jig**, **reel**, sword dance, clog dance, *mazurka* (folk dances), flamenco, country dance, waltz, polka, **ballet**, *pavane, galliard* (16th century)
friction drum, steel drums, bongos (small drums), congas (large drums), *timbales* (shallow drums), maracas (shakers), *guiro* (scraper)	toasting	*zouk* (pop music), tango, lambada, samba, *bossa nova* (city music), rumba, mambo, *merengue* (salsa)
tabla drum, *dhol* drum,, tambourine, *bartal* cymbals, bells, sticks, gongs	bards, *bhangra* (Punjabi), *qawwali* (Sufi music), throat singing, *ghazals* (love poems)	*bhangra, dabke* (traditional dances), Indian classical, whirling dervishes, belly dancing

Glossary

accordion musical instrument consisting of hand-held bellows, a keyboard, and reeds which produce musical notes. The keyboard is pressed, and the bellows are squeezed.

alphorn long wooden wind instrument. It has a cupped mouthpiece and the instrument ends in a horn, which projects the sound over long distances.

auditorium part of the concert hall where the audience sit

bagpipe wind instrument. The player blows into a sack that provides a constant flow of air. The melody is played on a stick called the chanter. A drone (single long note) accompanies the melody.

ballad folk song telling a story, or a slow pop song on the theme of love

ballet style of performance dance developed in the 17th century

bellows mechanical device for pumping air

brass instruments made of metal that are blown into. The sound is made by the lips vibrating in a mouthpiece.

castanets finger-held wooden percussion instruments from Spain

cell single room in which a person is expected to remain

Celtic people living on the western edge of Europe in parts of Britain, Ireland, France, and Spain, describe themselves as Celtic

Christianity one of the world's major religions, in which Jesus Christ is recognized as the son of God

clarinet wind instrument invented in the 18th century. The sound is produced by a reed vibrating when blown.

classical music music that is composed and written down. In the past it was mainly professional, trained musicians who would play, but it is now played by all kinds of people.

colony region or territory under the direct control of a distant country

composer person who writes music

concerto piece of music for orchestra, which features a solo instrument. For example, a piano concerto is written for piano and orchestra.

convent community of Christian nuns

empire group of nations or states ruled by a single nation

folk music music which is handed down in communities over many years. It is not usually written, but passed on by imitation and listening.

incense sweet-smelling smoke of dried plants, burned for religious ceremonies

Industrial Revolution time in the late 18th century when machinery began to replace manual labour

Islam one of the world's major religions. Its origins are in the Middle East. Its holy book is the Qur'an.

jig lively Irish dance

mass production making large numbers of identical products with machinery

Moors Muslim people from North Africa who occupied parts of Spain from the 8th to the 15th centuries

nomadic people who tend to move from place to place, rather than build permanent homes

orchestra large group of instruments played by trained musicians, usually grouped into woodwind, brass, strings, and percussion

pagan the worship of many gods, or of the natural world

pitch the "highness" or "lowness" of a note. A scream is generally high pitched, the rumble of thunder is low pitched.

plainchant type of religious chant often sung by monks

prodigy child who is able to achieve things that would be expected of someone much older

Protestant group of northern European Christians who broke away from the Roman Catholic Church in the 16th century

reel lively dance from the British Isles, particularly Scotland

reggae style of popular music from Jamaica

revolutionary when something is revolutionary it produces great change

rhythm the beat behind a piece of music

saint person who is regarded as holy. Christianity celebrates the lives of saints on certain days.

scale set of notes organized in regular upward or downward steps

score pages of written music

Soviet Union state made up of many countries in Eastern Europe, which existed between 1922 and 1991. Its centre was Russia.

steel band band from the Caribbean islands that uses oil drums as instruments

symphony long piece of music written for orchestra, usually in three or four sections

synthesizer electronic instrument capable of creating a very wide variety of sounds

tribute an act meant to show respect for someone. It is often for someone who has died.

woodwind instruments that are blown. The sound is either produced by vibrating reeds (clarinet), or by air vibrating over a hole (flute).

yodel style of singing from central Europe where the singer makes rapid changes of pitch from high to low sounds

Further information

Books

Europe (Rookie Read-About Geography), Allan Fowler (Children's Press, 2002)

Eurovision Song Contest: 50th Anniversary, John Kennedy O'Connor (Carlton, 2005)

The Beatles, Jeremy Roberts (Lerner, 2002)

The Handbook of the New Eastern Europe, Michael Kort (Millbrook Press, 2001)

Websites

BBC World Music
http://www.bbc.co.uk/music/world/

Classical Music Archives
http://www.classicalarchives.com/

East European Folklife Centre
http://www.eefc.org/site/

Folk and Roots Online Guide
http://www.folkworld.de/frog/index.html

Organizations

The European Music Office

http://www.musicineurope.org/

The European Music Office represents nearly all of Europe's music professionals, and promotes the diversity of European music throughout the world.

Places to visit

Cité de la Musique,
221 avenue Jean Jaurès, 75019 Paris, France
(Museum, exhibitions, and concerts)

Mozarts Geburtshaus, Getreidegasse 9, 5020 Salzburg, Austria
(Birthplace of Mozart)

Museu de la Música Barcelona,
C F Zona Franca 22, 08040 Barcelona, Spain
(Historic collection of Spanish instruments)

Museum of the Royal College of Music,
Prince Consort Road, London SW7 2BS
(Huge collection of instruments)

National Music Museum,
University of South Dakota, 414 East Clark Street, Vermillion, SD 57069
(Large collection of instruments)

Opera House of la Scala,
Milan, Italy
(An 18th-century opera house, and one of the most famous in the world)

The Beatles Story Experience,
Britannia Vaults, Albert Dock, Liverpool L3 4AD
(Visitor centre, tours, exhibitions)

Index